MW01601011

Your Life's Calling
Workbook

Maximizing What's Within to Engage Your Calling & Reach Your Destiny

Dr. Rhonda Thompson Alexander

Your Life's Calling Workbook: *Maximizing What's Within to Engage Your Calling & Reach Your Destiny*

By Rhonda Thompson Alexander

Visit the author's website: www.TheDrRhonda.com

Follow Dr. Rhonda on social media: @TheDrRhonda

Published by Rhonda Thompson Alexander for E² Executive & Entrepreneur Coaching, a division of IUVO Consulting, LLC, Virginia Beach, VA

Cover design by Photography by Mykahl Raphael

Follow on social media: @mykahlraphael

Online: www.MykahlRaphael.com

Trade paperback ISBN: 9781073133499

Contents

Introduction

Change is difficult. I'll be the first to admit that. The fact that you've chosen this workbook to accompany your copy of *Your Life's Calling: Maximizing What's Within to Engage Your Calling & Reach Your Goals*, however, makes a definitive statement that you are ready to make some major life changes. As I noted in the book, the pain of change is real, but I believe it's worth it if the result is a better, happier, more productive you! I believe your calling is meant to make you whole. In other words, it is intended to not only challenge and develop you, its purpose is also to satisfy you, provide for you, and bring significant meaning to your life.

Whether you're using this workbook as you read the main manuscript or if you've read the book already and are now preparing to do the work of change, the journey you're about to embark on is real. The person you're called to be is within you, just waiting to be birthed and put to use. As you provide the answers to the questions herein, be honest with yourself. You can't make real, lasting change if you're unwilling to face the hard truths about your life and your feelings. None of the questions or exercises will require you to show your answers to your friends and family, and no one will be looking over your shoulder. Even if you're using this workbook as a part of your coaching, you should not be afraid to be as open as necessary. The more open you are, the more likely you'll be to receive the insights you need to truly maximize what's within.

I hope that as you navigate through this workbook, you find the answers and help you're seeking. It is also my desire that this workbook would make a huge impact in your life and help you to become the person you're created and called to be!

How to Use This Workbook

This workbook is designed to be used in one of three ways

- It may be completed as you read *Your Life's Calling*
- It may be completed after you've read *Your Life's Calling*
- It may be completed as a coaching tool

As you read *Your Life's Calling*

This workbook follows the sequence of the book and can serve as a place to quickly jot down notes when you need to. The "insight" boxes in the margins, as well as the "Notes" boxes at the end of each of the workbook's chapters should help you keep track of your thoughts as you read and provide a space for you to note any insights you may receive, as well.

After Reading *Your Life's Calling*

Some individuals may need to spend time "taking in" what they read. They may not be able (or they may not want) to write as they read. In this case, the workbook serves as a great review of what you've read, which will help reinforce its principles and help you think more deeply about where you are and where you'd like to be in life. You may even find that you'll need to complete various parts of the workbook, especially Chapter 8, when you are experiencing certain challenges as you engage in and execute the work of your calling.

As A Coaching Tool

This is a great tool to work through with your entrepreneur coach. As a coach, I use it as a starting point for discussions intended to inspire my clients to think and act. Completing this workbook with a coach will help you stay motivated and accountable. Even better, you won't have to walk this transformative journey alone.

Part One

CHAPTER 1

The Call

1. Describe how your life has been spent doing work you felt you were *supposed* to do, instead of work you really enjoyed.

_____

_____

_____

_____

_____

_____

_____

_____

_____

_____

_____

_____

_____

_____

insight

_____

_____

_____

_____

_____

_____

_____

_____

_____

_____

_____

_____

_____

_____

_____

_____

2. What caused you to start that work? How long did you stick with it and why?

_____

_____

_____

_____

_____

_____

_____

_____

_____

_____

3. Which activities have you engaged in to try to "find yourself" or to discover the meaning of your life?

_____

_____

_____

_____

_____

_____

_____

_____

_____

_____

> "We encounter life-affirming and highly meaningful moments in our excursions of self-discovery, which make us *think* we've found the meaning of life, but in truth, our purpose in life continues to elude us."

4. In this chapter, I mentioned that we feel dissatisfied when we are working outside of our calling. In which aspects of your life do you feel dissatisfied or like something is missing?

_____

_____

_____

_____

_____

_____

_____

_____

5. Which of your life's memories stand out to you or caused you to make major pivots in your life?

_____

_____

_____

_____

_____

_____

_____

_____

_____

6. What are your "soap box" issues?

_____

_____

_____

_____

_____

_____

_____

_____

7. Where do you find yourself on
   Maslow's hierarchy of needs?
   What do you feel you need most
   at this time of your life?

Self Actualization
(the need for development, creativity)

Ego
(the need for self-esteem, power, recognition, prestige)

Social
(the need for being loved, belonging, inclusion)

Security
(the need for safety, shelter, stability)

Physical
(the need for air, water, food, rest, health)

_____

_____

_____

_____

_____

_____

_____

_____

_____

8. Do you feel your calling supersedes your current position in the hierarchy? How so? Think of concrete examples, if you can.

_____

_____

_____

_____

_____

_____

9. What is the book's definition of calling?

_____

_____

_____

_____

Complete this statement from the end of the chapter:

"When the reason you _____ combines with _____,

you create _____, which cause _____

and _____ to _____."

Your Life's Calling

NOTES

_____

_____

_____

_____

_____

_____

_____

_____

_____

_____

_____

_____

_____

_____

_____

CHAPTER 2

Who Is "Called"? (And Who Does the Calling?)

1. Are you one of the 87% of people who dislike or are disengaged at work?

   YES   NO

   If yes, what about your job do you dislike?

   _____

   _____

   _____

   _____

   _____

   _____

   _____

2. Do you often feel as though your financial obligations override your happiness? How does that ultimately make you feel about your work and yourself?

   _____

   _____

   _____

   _____

   _____

   _____

3. What would you do if you didn't have to work? What kind of person would you be? How would you feel? What would you become?

_____

_____

_____

_____

_____

_____

_____

_____

_____

_____

_____

_____

_____

_____

_____

_____

_____

_____

_____

_____

_____

_____

4. According to your belief system, what/who is the "external entity" that has called you?

_____

_____

_____

_____

_____

5. What do you believe to be your calling?

_____

_____

_____

_____

_____

_____

_____

_____

_____

_____

_____

_____

insight

_____

_____

_____

_____

_____

_____

_____

_____

_____

_____

_____

_____

_____

_____

_____

_____

_____

_____

_____

_____

_____

6. What are the 4 factors influencing calling?

_____   _____

_____   _____

NOTES

_____

_____

_____

_____

_____

_____

_____

_____

CHAPTER 3

Purpose

1. What is the definition of Purpose?

   _____

2. Do you remember when you started thinking about your purpose? How old were you? Was it in response to a specific event or season in your life?

   _____

   _____

   _____

   _____

   _____

   _____

   _____

3. List some of the self-help materials you've used to help you with the discovery of your Purpose. What did those items impart to you?

   _____

   _____

   _____

   _____

   _____

   _____

4. What is "ikigai"?

    _____

5. Finish this statement:

    "This means you are deliberate; your

    _____ is neither

    _____ nor

    _____."

6. What kind of work would you do, even if no one
    paid you to do it?

    _____

    _____

    _____

    _____

    _____

    _____

    _____

    _____

    _____

    _____

    _____

    _____

insight

_____

_____

_____

_____

_____

_____

_____

_____

_____

_____

_____

_____

_____

_____

_____

_____

_____

_____

_____

_____

_____

_____

7. Who do you believe you are created to be?

_____

_____

_____

8. Finish this statement found at the end of the chapter:

"This is our Purpose: the space for which we were _____ _____

and where we fill a _____ inaccessible to _____

_____.

NOTES

_____

_____

_____

_____

_____

_____

_____

CHAPTER 4

Passion

1. What is the definition of Passion?

    _____

    _____

2. Which type(s) of work, activities or tasks could you engage in for hours?

    _____

    _____

    _____

    _____

    _____

    _____

    _____

    _____

    _____

    _____

    _____

3. Finish this statement:

"Your Purpose is meant_____, but your

Passion is meant _____."

4. True or False: The work that makes you smile and the work which serves your Purpose cannot be the same.

TRUE   FALSE

5. How do you feel when you're engaged in work you're passionate about? What kind of stamina and tenacity do you have in those times?

_____

_____

_____

_____

_____

_____

_____

_____

_____

_____

_____

_____

6. Describe a scenario or season where the joy of your work was "leaking" out of your life. Describe how that made you feel.

_____

_____

_____

_____

_____

_____

_____

_____

_____

7. Core values are the fundamental beliefs which help you define and differentiate between right and wrong. Some examples are the belief that honesty is always the best policy or that people should "do good" for others or live healthy, balanced lives. What are your core values?

_____

_____

_____

_____

_____

_____

_____

_____

_____

8. Why do you do your work?

_____

_____

_____

_____

_____

_____

_____

_____

9. According to the book, what percentage of your happiness will come from money, fame, or status?

_____

NOTES

_____

_____

_____

_____

_____

_____

CHAPTER 5

Performance

1. What is the definition of Performance?

_____

_____

2. What's the difference between the definition of Passion and Performance?

_____

_____

_____

_____

3. Finish these statements:

The degree to which you are passionate and

purposeful can only be _____

by you and _____ by

others. Your Performance, however, can be

_____ and _____

by others _____.

4. Which lessons have you learned from your work history above and beyond concrete skills?

_____

_____

_____

_____

_____

5. How have you evolved in your work?

_____

_____

_____

_____

_____

_____

_____

_____

6. Describe an occasion when you were working hard but making no progress. How did you feel during that time?

_____

_____

_____

_____

_____

_____

7. Describe a time when you excelled "unexpectedly."

_____

_____

_____

_____

_____

8. Finish this statement:

"The fear of _____ is likely to

be the most _____

_____ to your ability to walk

fully in your calling."

What are SMART goals relating to your work?

S _____

M _____

A _____

R _____

T _____

9. What's the biggest accomplishment you've achieved thus far in your life?

_____

_____

_____

_____

_____

10. Your comfort zone consists of the people, places, and things, which represent stability and security. It is also what keeps most people from taking the risks necessary to make major life changes. Which things make up *your* comfort zone? What impact are they having on your ability to fully walk in your calling?

_____

_____

_____

_____

_____

_____

_____

_____

_____

_____

_____

_____

_____

_____

_____

_____

_____

_____

_____

NOTES

_____

_____

_____

_____

_____

_____

_____

_____

_____

_____

_____

_____

_____

_____

_____

_____

CHAPTER 6

Progress

1. What is the book's definition of Progress?

   _____

2. What are some of the major struggles you've had in life?

   _____

   _____

   _____

   _____

   _____

   _____

   _____

   _____

   Complete this statement:

   "To produce progress, your work should change the way people _____ or _____."

3. What are some of the major victories you've experienced in your life?

   _____

   _____

   _____

   _____

   _____

4. Are there any aspects of your work which continue to be effective long after you've finished? If so, what are they and how are they perpetually effective?

_____

_____

_____

_____

_____

_____

_____

_____

5. What role does love play in your work when it comes to your ability to impact and influence others?

_____

_____

_____

_____

_____

_____

_____

_____

6. Finish the following statement:

"Progress begins when we realize that our called work is to be used for the

_____, and not for _____."

7. How does your work allow you to serve others?

_____

_____

_____

_____

_____

_____

_____

_____

NOTES

_____

_____

_____

_____

_____

_____

_____

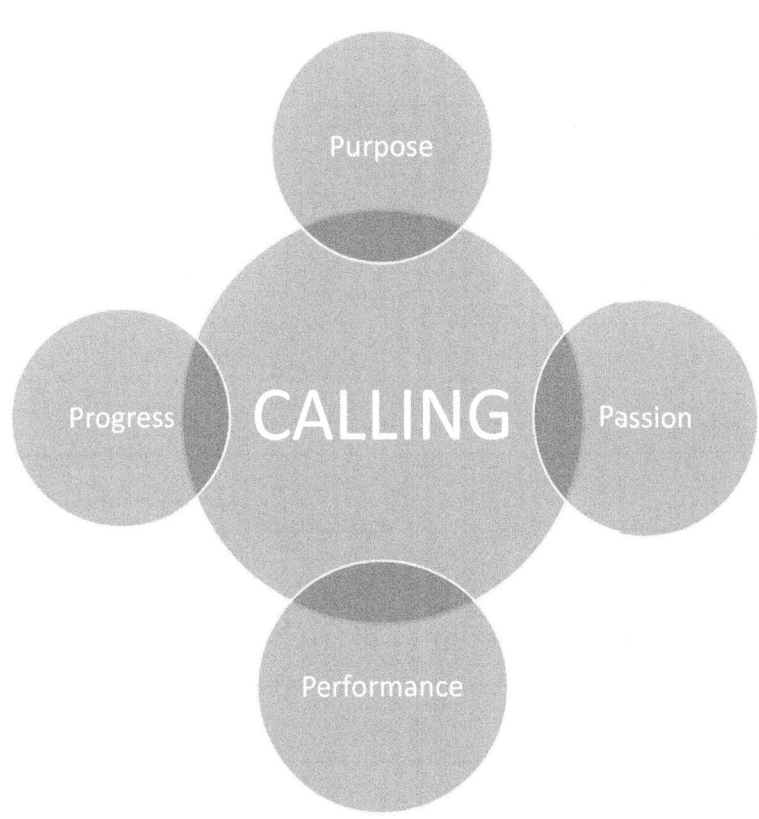

Part Two

CHAPTER 7

The 4Ps of Your Calling

Your **Purpose** reflects the ways you use your effectiveness to impact those around you. Your effectiveness (or the work you do well) is comprised of the skills and expertise you've acquired over the years, whether through your education or the honing of your natural talents. The impact you have on others is connoted by the legacy you're currently working to leave or the legacy you desire to leave.

Purpose = How you impact others + Your effectiveness

Passion is the work you love to do, coupled with a high motivation to do it. The motivation driving passion is *intrinsic,* meaning it is its own reward. The work you love to do is that which you can become completely engrossed, such that you lose track of time, or that which you feel a strong urge or need to do.

Passion = The work you love + Your intrinsic motivation to do it

The **Performance** factor reflects your areas of effectiveness, as described above, combined with the *extrinsic* motivators driving you. Extrinsic motivators are external to you, and include rewards like praise, awards, and accolades. They are "things" individuals strive to receive or achieve for work performed well.

Performance = Your effectiveness + Your extrinsic motivators (rewards)

The **Progress** you affect on society is a result of the influence or impact you have on others while doing work you love. As noted above, your impact can be actual or intended, but it is manifested through work you're currently doing.

Progress = How you impact others + The work you love

As you answer the following questions, consider the work you're doing *now*. Even if you're describing your legacy in terms of what you desire to leave behind, consider the work you're doing today, which contributes to that desired legacy.

<u>*Your Effectiveness*</u>

1. In which type of work, tasks, or activities do you consider yourself to be most effective?

    _____

    _____

    _____

    _____

    _____

    _____

2. To which pieces of concrete data can you turn to confirm your perceived effectiveness? Recall the specifics: number of "things" sold, times quota was exceeded, quantity of people helped, etc. You should include numbers, if you can.

    _____

    _____

    _____

    _____

    _____

    _____

    _____

What You Enjoy

3. Which types of work, tasks, or activities do you enjoy and why? (This can include answers extending beyond your employment.)

_____

_____

_____

_____

_____

_____

_____

_____

_____

4. How often do you permit yourself to engage in the activities you enjoy? How do you feel while you're immersed in them?

_____

_____

_____

_____

_____

_____

_____

_____

_____

<u>*Your Motivators*</u>

5. What are your intrinsic motivators (the internal driver that makes you *want* to do certain types of work)?

_____

_____

_____

_____

_____

_____

_____

_____

_____

6. What are your extrinsic motivators (the rewards and accolades you've achieved or desire to attain)?

_____

_____

_____

_____

_____

_____

_____

_____

<u>*Your Impact*</u>

7. How do you positively influence or impact others?

_____

_____

_____

_____

_____

_____

_____

_____

_____

8. What is the impact you'd ultimately like to have on the people who encounter you and your work?

_____

_____

_____

_____

_____

_____

_____

_____

_____

The 4P Model

Use this section to summarize your answers to the eight questions above. Enter them into the corresponding boxes, to determine how your entries in each quadrant either comprise or contribute to your Purpose, Passion, Progress, and Performance.

YOUR <u>IMPACT</u>	WHAT YOU <u>ENJOY</u>	
		PROGRESS
YOUR <u>EFFECTIVENESS</u> **CALLING**	YOUR <u>MOTIVATORS</u>	
	Intrinsic	
		PERFORMANCE
	Extrinsic	
PURPOSE	PASSION	

Now that you've filled in the model, how do your responses reflect your perceived Purpose, Passion, Performance, and Progress? Where do gaps between your current work and your called work seem to appear? Are there "overlaps" or areas of your current work that are already aligned with your calling?

Purpose

How well are the components aligned?

_____
_____
_____
_____

Gaps

_____
_____
_____
_____

Overlaps

_____
_____
_____
_____

Passion

How well are the components aligned?

_____

_____

_____

_____

_____

Gaps

_____

_____

_____

_____

_____

Overlaps

_____

_____

_____

_____

_____

Performance

How well are the components aligned?

_____

_____

_____

_____

_____

Gaps

_____

_____

_____

_____

_____

Overlaps

_____

_____

_____

_____

_____

Progress

How well are the components aligned?

_____

_____

_____

_____

_____

Gaps

_____

_____

_____

_____

_____

Overlaps

_____

_____

_____

_____

_____

CHAPTER 8

Aligning the 4Ps of your Calling

This part of the workbook is meant to help you resolve some of the common symptoms experienced by people whose work is misaligned with their calling. You may not need to complete all sections at once; instead, you may find that this part of the workbook will be useful during various periods of your life when you feel as though you're not as effective or efficient in the work of your calling as you desire. As stated in the book, the fact that only four symptoms are presented does not mean that these are the only ones you can possibly experience, nor does it mean you will definitely experience any or all of them.

After completing the exercise in Chapter 8, how do you feel about the alignment between your life's work and your calling?

_____

_____

_____

_____

_____

_____

_____

_____

SYMPTOM 1: Feeling "stuck" – The Lack of Enjoyment

Individuals who feel stuck likely have a sense of their Purpose (and know they're not operating in it fully), and their Performance has been historically high. Their lack of Passion and Progress, however, takes a toll and leaves these individuals with the strong desire to do something they love and to be engaged in work which cause them to evolve. The strongest desires in these individuals are to grow, develop, and thrive and to regain their zeal for life and their work.

Questions to help you address this symptom:

1.   What, if anything, do I love about my current work?

_____

_____

_____

_____

_____

2.   What has made me feel so comfortable doing work I dislike?

_____

_____

_____

_____

_____

_____

_____

3.   Which type(s) of work would get me out of bed, smiling and looking forward
       to each day?

_____

_____

_____

_____

_____

_____

_____

_____

_____

_____

_____

_____

_____

_____

_____

_____

_____

_____

_____

_____

SYMPTOM 2: "Meaningless Existence" – The Lack of Impact

People who feel their existence is meaningless are usually engaged in work which hasn't gotten into their heart. They feel their work has lost its impact. No matter how enjoyable it is, or how effective they may be in performing their work, they cannot continue it for long because neither they nor those around them seem to be better as a result of it.

Questions to help you address this symptom:

1. How does my work make others' lives better?

_____

_____

_____

_____

_____

_____

_____

2. Which causes or agendas are supported by the work I do?

_____

_____

_____

_____

_____

3. Use this page to create your epitaph or eulogy. Write about yourself as though you were no longer here, reflecting on all you've done for yourself, your family, your community, and society to date. What will you say regarding your influence? How did your contributions to society, in turn, affect you?

_____

_____

_____

_____

_____

_____

_____

_____

_____

_____

_____

_____

_____

_____

_____

_____

_____

_____

_____

_____

SYMPTOM 3: "Floundering" – The Lack of Effectiveness

People in this category feel that, perhaps, they have no calling: they're just alive to serve or take up space. The perception of their work and their existence is quite negative, because they haven't settled on their life's Purpose, nor are they able to perceive any real accomplishments in their life. Even if they enjoy the types of work they take on, people who are floundering tend to feel they are consistently held back from reaching desired achievements, or they perceive that success is just outside their reach.

Questions to help you address this symptom:

1. What am I good at? Which things do I do *well*? Keep in mind, this may not relate to your employment alone. Think about your response from a holistic perspective.

_____

_____

_____

_____

_____

_____

_____

_____

_____

_____

_____

2. On which occasions (or for which reasons) was I told "Great Job" or received similar recognition or praise?

_____

_____

_____

_____

_____

_____

_____

_____

3. Are there "soft skills," qualities, or traits for which I've been recognized?

_____

_____

_____

_____

_____

_____

_____

_____

_____

_____

4. I was extremely proud of myself when...

_____

_____

_____

_____

_____

_____

_____

_____

_____

_____

_____

_____

_____

_____

_____

_____

_____

_____

_____

_____

_____

_____

_____

5. Review your resumé, not for the purpose of finding a new job, but to consider what you've taken away from each position you've worked, whether you considered your Performance to be high in those roles or not. Give a good, long look at each job you've held and recall what you brought to the table, as well as what you received in return. Yes, you received something from each one, beyond your paycheck, which added to the value of your work. Remind yourself how you employed those increases to improve your level of effectiveness in various areas.

_____

_____

_____

_____

_____

_____

_____

_____

_____

_____

_____

_____

_____

_____

_____

_____

_____

_____

_____

SYMPTOM 4: "Burned Out" – The Lack of Motivation

Burned out individuals are clear on Purpose, and they can be highly productive. Strangely, however, they still find it hard to get out of bed each day to do the work they know is important. In this case, their Passion is gone, over time, their Performance declines. Ultimately, these individuals find themselves lacking what it takes to give their work their all.

Questions to help you address this symptom:

1. Which aspects of my work drain me?

   _____

   _____

   _____

   _____

   _____

   _____

   _____

2. Which aspects of my work or life give me energy or make me feel revived?

   _____

   _____

   _____

   _____

   _____

   _____

   _____

3. Why am I doing my work?

_____

_____

_____

_____

_____

_____

_____

_____

_____

_____

4. If I could quit my work today, with no repercussions, I would…

_____

_____

_____

_____

_____

_____

_____

_____

_____

_____

Becoming Aligned

In which category do you find yourself?

_____

_____

Are there any life changes you consider necessary at this point?

_____

_____

_____

_____

_____

_____

_____

What steps can you take in the next 10 days to begin making the changes you noted above?

1. _____

2. _____

3. _____

4. _____

5. _____

6. _____

7. _____

Extra Notes or Thoughts